# 31 Secr

# A Successful

# Marriage

## Matthew Ashimolowo

MATTYSON MEDIA

© **1998 Matthew Ashimolowo**

Mattyson Media Company
P. O. Box 12961
London
E15 1UR

Bible quotes are from the King James Bible unless otherwise stated.

ISBN 1-874646-22-8

# Contents

# Introduction

Marriage has been called the *"great institution"* but modern man has made it look like the *"great mistake"*. We live at a time when marriage the great expectation of all humanity now results in the unexpected.

When you look at the statistics of marriage, in the United Kingdom for example, the statistics are grim. One in three homes is led by a single parent. We did not have such a picture when God first instituted marriage.

Divorce has risen by more than sixty-eight per cent since the Sixties. Every year, seventy thousand separations take place in the United Kingdom alone the highest rate being amongst those who are living together.

Eighteen thousand teenagers get pregnant every year. To complicate matters, television, radio, newspapers, magazines, in fact, all aspects of the media now affect the moral fabric of society. It belittles the institution of marriage, berates the church, exalts infidelity and promotes the *"living together thing"*, making a mockery of virginity.

**Is successful marriage possible?**

**Can marriages really be healthy?**

The answer will be an absolute YES. Firstly based on Scripture, secondly based on principles derived from it and thirdly because we are surrounded by a cloud of witnesses of those who are making a success out of their marriage despite the grim statistics. Marriage is still popular, with over two hundred thousand taking place in the United Kingdom annually. The number of those getting married is still higher than those getting a divorce.

It is my sincere desire, hope, prayer and expectation that the next thirty one secrets will bless your life, challenge you, cause you to be victorious and focused in raising a successful marriage.

# # I

# Successful Marriages Pursue Intimacy

Joe and Donna were childhood friends; they met at a teenage party and from then were inseparable. It was love at first sight. By the time they sat across the table from me in counselling, with two children between them, they had been through so much fighting. The childhood flame, which had started the relationship, had long gone out. It had probably been kindled by the mutual need they both had. Both came from broken homes, with abuses and similar hurts, but having come together, reality began to dawn that two broken people don't make a whole marriage.

Their story is not unique; it doesn't take long to know a marriage that lacks intimacy. There are several pointers. In such a marriage you hear them fight if you live next door. It is their regular pastime and even in casual conversations they are busy interrupting one another. When matters, which require discussion, come up, it is a major debate, with each raising their voice as if they have to win the argument to be the head in the marriage.

In marriages that lack intimacy there is no sensitivity to one another. The other person's needs are not the paramount motivation for action but rather something to take advantage of. The dysfunctional marriage cannot be called a companionship. The couple do not see each other as two fellows who are meant to make the boat in which they find themselves work. On the contrary they are on each other's case, and as a result of the incessant fighting the emotional glue needed to make the marriage stay together is missing.

So Joe and Donna ended up as co-tenants under one roof, experiencing loneliness in the place where there should be intimacy. The unfortunate thing is that their backgrounds do not equip them with the skills to handle the dysfunction in their marriage. Unless they realise that they share mutual pain and must learn to develop mutual love they are likely to stay in their state of pain.

Joe and Donna also come from dysfunctional homes. We never seem to totally move from the home of our upbringing. If we do, it has to be a deliberate act. A person from a dysfunctional home must acknowledge that fact and make an effort to build a marriage that will succeed; but the journey certainly is not easy.

Through bad mentoring, they have observed only the negatives of marriage and although brought together by hearts on fire the poor examples they have seen and the poor teachings they have had have now complicated matters for them.

All cases are not as bad as Joe and Donna's. For every Joe and Donna there are several success stories, as in the case of Pete and Valerie. When you see them in church, out of church, on the street or catch them unawares, the intimacy they seem to beam out in the way they are holding hands, talking intimately, laughing, smiling, looking into each other's eyes, gives you the impression that they are probably putting on a public display of affection. But drawing closer and listening to their story you will know that something deeper and greater has brought both together.

If you ever have a reason to interview Pete and Valerie, the ingredients that make up an intimate marriage are immediately noticeable, the first among them being:

An intense affection for the Lord Jesus Christ, the one who has brought them together. True marriages that will experience and keep intimacy must maintain intimacy that is motivated by their mutual love for the Lord.

This then develops into mutual affection for one another. Affection is easily displayed during courtship. The man by nature is the pursuant; the woman by nature is the respondent. Unfortunately after courtship, the hunter is likely to take his prey for granted.

When you listen to Pete and Valerie you can tell obviously that they do have points of differences but despite that they never get into shouting contests. Rather they sit in conference to settle differences ensuring that no stone is left unturned. No subject is too sacred to be discussed. They are ready to open up until they both find catharsis for whatever wound has come from relating to one another.

It is also very easy to notice, as in the case of Pete and Valerie, that there is a lot of laughter, not because they have everything they ever wanted, but because they have found satisfaction in sharing fellowship with one another and in their relationship. They see marriage as a place where each other's strength is to be emphasised because whatever you denigrate and put down never gets better. On the contrary they build up one another both in the presence of other people and while with each other. You could never build intimacy with a person who puts you down. They also choose to emphasise the positive sides of each other. Human nature easily recognises weaknesses but people become better in the area we choose to emphasis. In intimate marriages there is also mutual sharing with each other, which leads to a positive interaction in all matters of marriage.

How do you take your marriage forward? How do you bring the extra into your ordinary to make your marriage sparkle and stronger? There are a number of steps you can take:

It is not enough to feel affection for your spouse: It needs to be shown. When the other person knows that they are cared for and appreciated they go to all lengths to also express the same. Many marriages will mature and be better if people do not selfishly pursue their own ends but seek the best for their spouse.

**Perform acts of caring:** There are certainly actions that indicate that we care for the other person. Asking them for major and minor things that relate to their life taking particular note to surprise them with TLC (*tender loving care*).

**Show appreciation:** It is a miracle for somebody of a totally different background to choose to live with you. Appreciate the good things about them and let them know what you value about them. If all they hear is complaining the marriage can never be intimate, neither are they able to open up in the area where they need help.

**Shared interests:** Marriages where their interests are different can never be intimate. In a marriage where the husband faces the north and the wife south they can never arrive at the same conclusion.

**Do not take each other for granted:** This is very easy, especially as the years go by. The man comes home in the evening and he meets warm food on the table and maybe his wife is the traditional type who irons his shirts, she prepares the children for school and at the same time still performs her function as a wife. It is possible for him to take her for granted because he is insensitive to her. He just considers those things as her duty. On the other hand there is the wife who thinks it is her husband's responsibility to provide and she does not consider any steps he has taken as being unusual.

**Avoid the criticism trap:** It is so easy to drift into this spirit and pull one another down. Whatever we refuse to build up but end up tearing down never grows. This particular style or action of criticism opens the door for other destructive responses, critical jokes, humour that does not build. All these contribute to weakening a marriage.

Remember above everything that your marriage is intended for mutual affection and for greater joy and as you contribute all you have, you will not join the statistics of broken marriages. You must be vertical in your relationship with God, praying together, talking to God together and horizontal in your relationship with your wife, being intimate, sharing fellowship, building one another and making sure one another's dreams become mutual and fulfilling.

# # 2

# Successful Marriages Have A Workable Method Of Resolving Conflicts

*"A soft answer turneth away wrath: but grievous words stir up anger."*
*Proverbs 15:1*

*Let no corrupt communication proceed out of your mouth, but that which is good to the use of edifying, that it may minister grace unto the hearers.*

*And grieve not the Holy Spirit of God, whereby ye are sealed unto the day of redemption.*

*Let all bitterness, and wrath, and anger,*

> *and clamor, and evil speaking, be put*
> *away from you, with all malice."*
> *Ephesians 4:29-31*

When two people come together in holy matrimony, it's more like two aliens who discovered each other. Their backgrounds are different and therefore they are likely to see things in certain respects in a different way. The interesting thing about marriage is that we are attracted to our spouses for things that are similar and for things that are different. Conflicts therefore do come between couples but it is important to not feed conflicts with reactions that are not helpful. So

**Avoid assumptions**. Assumption in my opinion is the mother of mess-ups. Whenever we assume, we take actions, conclude matters and end up hurting our partners.

**Do not refer to the past.** Reference to the past only complicates conflict resolution. Anything older than six months is now the past. That is why matters should be resolved as soon as they come up.

## Aim to resolve not to win.

> *"He that handleth a matter wisely shall find good: and whoso trusteth in the LORD, happy is he." Proverbs 16:20*

Conflict resolution is not a place to gain victory and after all if you win in an argument with your spouse, to whom would you announce your victory?

Do not describe your spouse's state of being as a permanent character trait. This is another major step in conflict resolution. It is very tempting to use language like *"you are always doing this"*, *"you are always hurting me"*, *"you are fond of doing this"*. For them to always do it, they would have to do it twenty-four hours a day and for three hundred sixty-five days a year. Furthermore, recognise that the devil hates your marriage, particularly if it is a marriage founded on Christ, so not all of your conflicts and problems are the products of differences. The enemy hates you and wants to create conflicts.

In the process of resolving conflicts, some matters will be important to your spouse. If they are, they deserve discussion. You cannot avoid discussion. The only time you can deflect discussion is if both of you are still angry or one of you is still angry. This means that as soon as both of you feel that your temper or feeling can accommodate honest open discussion, it should take place.

In resolving conflicts you have got to know that conflicts come when we expect our spouses to know things automatically. We just do not give them enough information and wonder why they do not know what they ought to have known; but how will they know if they were not informed?

Furthermore, in resolving conflict, to keep your marriage healthy, be willing to make-up first. Be willing to open the line of communication first, even if you feel you were the one offended.

Remember that it is better to acquire the skill for restoring your marriage than for winning because it is better for you to restore your spouse than for you to win an argument.

There are godly ways to resolve matters. A godly solution will consider the need of the two sides.

*"Through wisdom is an house builded;
and by understanding it is established:*

*And by knowledge shall the chambers
be filled with all precious and pleasant
riches.*

*A wise man is strong; yea, a man of
knowledge increaseth strength."*
*Proverb 24:3-5*

Do not always look at matters purely from your
own perspective. Your spouse has one and it
matters a lot.

Conflict resolution is much easier in an
atmosphere of a honest marriage where both
have concluded that *"we agree to disagree"*. In
other words, you have agreed to have points of
disagreement. You have agreed to not force
your opinion on your spouse.

So, learn to deal with the issues one at a time in
resolving conflicts. Do not come up with three or
four points to discuss. Each point is major to itself
and may only result in added conflict and further
argument. Conflicts cannot remain if you discuss
regularly and openly. Therefore, tie this with one
other point, which is communication. Do not take

on the role of a psychologist or an archaeologist in your marriage.

**Psychologists try to understand what is on people's minds or what is wrong with people's minds.** Whenever you drift into saying to your spouse *"I know what you are thinking"*, *"I know what is on your mind"*, *"I know you so well because I have always lived with you"*, *"I know what you can do"*, *"I know why you did this"*, you have already assumed the position of a psychologist and may be dreadfully wrong.

**Archaeologists dig up the past.** Whenever you bring up a person's past, what it says to them is that it is not forgiven or forgotten. You can only make progress as you willingly release the past and look forward to the future. The greatest enemy to the future is the past.

Conflicts are never resolved in the atmosphere of blackmail, so do not use your emotions to blackmail your spouse, particularly when you are tempted to say *"you do not love me anymore"*, *"you have never loved me"*, *"you do not care about me"*. Those are very powerful statements and they pierce the heart of our spouses, because they do not fully reflect the other person's feeling. They are conclusions which we have made and could be dreadfully wrong.

# #3

# Successful Marriages Have Mentors They Look Up To, To Challenge Them To A Better Marriage

We are surrounded by mentors:

➲ lateral mentors, who are our mates,

➲ downward mentors, people who look up to us,

➲ upward mentors, people we look up to.

Your marriage needs those you can look up to,

those from whom you can learn. Paul in writing to Timothy said, *"Be ye imitators of me, as I am of Christ"*. In other words there are things in his life, which he feels others can learn from.

Be ready to learn from positive marriages, those you can look up to who seem to have their marriage together. Ask them questions; be frank. Sit down with marriages that challenge you. Do not wait until there is a breakdown in your marriage before you seek help. Healthy marriages are sometimes products of the environment, that is, other marriages. Be open to your mentors. Be vulnerable to them. Ask them to criticise if possible or to shed light on areas that are not clear to you. Go to relationship seminars together with your spouse; look for places where marriage seminars are held. Grow together. Be friends of one another as you learn and observe from other people's lives.

Mentors are necessary because mentors are already in the future. They are already acting out what we are thinking about. They are already practising what we are planning. Mentors see the future while we see the present.

If your spouse does not put a great esteem on the need for mentoring, he or she may not put a great esteem on you. A person who is not ready to learn from others will become a little island, drift away and carry his marriage along into a lot of wrongs.

Look also for good family models that can help you as you shape together a home. Ask those who have raised champion kids how they did it in a world that is falling apart. Do not just assume that because you know the Bible, you already have it together.

Progress in life is a product of learning from others. Paul said;

> *"and that you have heard and seen*
> *of me, the same commit to others."*
> *II Timothy 2:2*

# *#4*

# Successful Marriages Do Not Take Each Other For Granted

It is important to know that when you bring another person into your life, the vows you made to share the future together are important and need to be observed. If you take your wife for granted or your husband, you provoke them to act in a way that may be challenging for you in the future.

William Shakespeare said *"hell hath no fury like a woman scorned"*. None of us like to be taken for granted, overlooked and treated as if we are an addendum or a problem. Therefore, explore one another, spirit, soul and body. Explore your spouse. Get to know them spiritually, get to know how they feel in their personality.

A spouse just wants to know that you care and you can only show that you care by leaving all others and cleaving only onto them. The Bible says

> *"And the LORD God caused a deep sleep to fall upon Adam, and he slept: and he took one of his ribs, and closed up the flesh instead thereof;*
>
> *And the rib, which the LORD God had taken from man, made he a woman, and brought her unto the man.*
>
> *And Adam said, This is now bone of my bones, and flesh of my flesh: she shall be called Woman, because she was taken out of Man.*
>
> *Therefore shall a man leave his father and his mother, and shall cleave unto his wife: and they shall be one flesh.*
>
> *And they were both naked, the man and his wife, and were not ashamed."*
> *Genesis 2:21-25*

It is important that you really do leave everything in your past and cleave. Prepare to leave what you have and cleave to whom you have now gotten married to. You cannot cleave if you do not leave. Drop the old boyfriend or girlfriend, drop the image of the abusive father and let mummy know it is over. Do not let imaginary partners come to your new bed with you. Furthermore, you need to understand that your wife just wants a sensitive man who cares for her and wants to build a future of victory.

> *"So ought men to love their wives as their own bodies. He that loveth his wife loveth himself.*
>
> *For no man ever yet hated his own flesh; but nourisheth and cherisheth it, even as the Lord the church."*
> *Ephesians 5:28-29*

In the same token, a man feels very high if his wife holds him in high esteem. Men had position before they had relationship. When they are taken for granted, it hurts deeply. A good number of men become abusive and wife beaters, purely because the wife has taken for granted the man she vowed to respect and honour.

Above all remember that you need to make the

best of having each other. Many who have gone down the road of divorce have later found that what they got married to a second or third time could not be compared to what they lost.

# #5

# Their Lines Of Communication Are Open And Clear

Marriage can be strong or weak. It can be a place of joy or problem, it can be filled with bliss or blisters. One particular area where marriages can be very strong and which couples need to work on is their communication. In other words, couples need to talk a lot and to keep talking. Where there is the absence of open communication, assumptions come up and hurt the marriage.

Communication can be positive or negative. Negative communication destroys relationships, hurts the marriage and makes the other person feel unwanted. Therefore, all negatives need to be weeded out. The less negative feedback will help both to move forward.

Some of the ways to achieve positive communication is by learning to hear the heart of your spouse without responding until they have finished. Furthermore, expressing your feeling or opinion, which may be different from theirs in a loving way, will help your marriage to grow.

Nobody really wants to wake up to create a destructive atmosphere in his or her marriage. It is where people misunderstand each other that they become suspicious of one another's motives and therefore hurt each other further. Effective communication in marriage means feelings must be responded to with feelings and acts with fact.

In your marriage, the times will come when provocation will cause you to want to say the wrong things. Speak positively into your marriage; confess good things about the future of your relationship. Take divorcing, dividing and departure to be "*D*" words, which must not be used in your marriage.

⮑ Divorcing means breaking apart what has been put together.

⮑ Dividing means severing two people who are meant to be together.

⮑ Departure means denying your spouse their conjugal sexual rights.

Be particular about the words you use. Make sure they are building blocks and not destructive words.

> *"Let no corrupt communication proceed out of your mouth, but that which is good to the use of edifying, that it may minister grace unto the hearers."*
> *Ephesians 4:29*

Earlier on I wrote that you should talk a lot. Do not just talk, communicate. Make sure you open your heart up to your spouse and if they are not hearing you well and the marriage is falling apart, it might just be healthy to bring in a third party who will be mature enough to set both of you in motion on the road to effective communication.

The word communication comes from

communing. Marriage is really the common union or communion of two people. To communicate therefore is to make the common union work. Remember and recognise the impact of non-verbal communication in your marriage also. It is not what we say that often hurts people but how it is said. The tone of voice, eye contact, the facial expression and the lack of interest have their impact in marital communication. If your communication has reached a dead end and hurtful exchanges are now taking place and argument become repeated over matters of little importance, you need to get to the root of the communication breakdown. Bring healing to it so you can move on with your marriage. Always remember that the place of communication is the place of health.

# *#6*

# Successful Marriages Place A High Value On Praying Together And For Each Other

*"Likewise, ye husbands, dwell with them according to knowledge, giving honour unto the wife, as unto the weaker vessel, and as being heirs together of the grace of life; that your prayers be not hindered." I Peter 3:7*

*"If two of you shall agree together concerning anything." Matthew 18:19*

We say *"the family which prays together stays together"*. How this chemistry works is a mystery but certainly even in our relationship with other people, we find that we do not gossip about those for whom we pray and we do not pray for those about whom we gossip. A family, which prays together, is not easily divided or defeated.

First, there is a spiritual dimension to the marriage and there is an unseen third party in the marriage who is going to make it work because it is to him we address our prayer and only he can adjudicate in matters that have to do with our life. Marriages will be healthy as we build our lives around an altar. A family altar is not an option but a must. There are challenges, pressures of life and opportunities which will confront your home which you cannot win with your natural strength, for the scriptures says *"by strength shall no man prevail"*. The family altar should therefore be strongly built and where it has been broken down, it needs to be revived.

The enemy will perpetually attack your family altar and cause both of you to make comments like *"Pray on your own and I will pray on my own"*. It is important to pray with one another and to pray for one another. Let a lot of your praying be in the Spirit. Learning to draw the dynamic power of the Holy Spirit into your family life is so important. Apart form the regular family devotions, spend quality time in prayer for your spouse. Pray for their vision, their dreams, their fulfilment and for what they always wanted.

If a family prays in agreement, it will set miracles in motion and while you are doing that, remember that the scripture is very particular about your spouse and your prayer. Nothing closes the windows of heaven like unkindness to your spouse.

> *"And this have ye done again, covering the altar of the LORD with tears, with weeping, and with crying out, insomuch that he regardeth not the offering any more, or receiveth it with good will at your hand.*
>
> *"Yet ye say, Wherefore? Because the LORD hath been witness between thee and the wife of thy youth, against whom thou hast dealt treacherously: yet is she thy companion, and the wife of thy covenant." Malachi 2:13-14*

> *Likewise, ye husbands, dwell with them according to knowledge, giving honour unto the wife, as unto the weaker vessel, and as being heirs together of the grace of life; that your prayers be not hindered." I Peter 3:7*

Do not let your family's destiny, future and prayer be hindered. Pray together and pray for one another to gain the victory, which God has designed for you.

# #7

# Successful Spouses Share A Common Interest, Friendship And Worldview

It is hard for two people in a marriage, when one is facing the east while the other is facing the west, to come to the same conclusion. Where worldviews are opposing and interests differ, with the couple having different friends and relationships, marriage can never be well bonded. They will both be like petrol and water; they will never mix.

Taking your marriage into oneness in worldview, friendships and interests will mean showing interest in what your spouse likes and running with the same ideas. Furthermore, venerate, value and adore your spouse in public. Let the world know you are proud of your spouse or particularly your wife or husband. It does a lot of good when the other person in the marriage knows that you appreciate them.

Having brought this person into your life, it is important to prioritise your relationship with him or her above everyone else.

> *"And the rib, which the LORD God had taken from man, made he a woman, and brought her unto the man.*
>
> *And Adam said, This is now bone of my bones, and flesh of my flesh: she shall be called Woman, because she was taken out of Man.*
>
> *Therefore shall a man leave his father and his mother, and shall cleave unto his wife: and they shall be one flesh."*
> *Genesis 2:22-24*

A lot of people just want to be sure that they are loved and cared for. Showing an interest in what your spouse likes will give the feeling of being deeply loved. If you pursue their interest, you make them your life partner for life. When a couple's hearts are knit to a common cause, in other words, not opposing views, friendships, relationships and interests, you would experience a bonding difficult to break up.

Successful marriages and successful couples place a high value on their relationship with God. You cannot operate outside your belief system. What your convictions are concerning God, the scriptures, the future and eternity does shape how you behave and how you run your life. It is therefore important for a couple to make sure that they do not have different worldviews when it comes to that which is spiritual. They need to consolidate a relationship with God, building into their family convictions, which will give the whole of their future a foundation. They hold a conviction as regards worshipping together.

> *"Not forsaking the assembling of ourselves together, as the manner of some is; but exhorting one another: and so much the more, as ye see the day approaching." Hebrews 10:25*

If the man is convinced that he does not need

church and the wife has a conviction that she has to go the mid-week and Sunday services, arguments will always come up. As a pastor, one of the most grieving experiences is how many marriages you know would have done well but their biggest argument is in the area of their spiritual life. There is a need to settle matters related to quiet time, praying together and who would lead the prayer time in the family or who is responsible for worship.

What are the purposes of family devotion in your opinion?

> *"Hear, O Israel: The LORD our God is one LORD:*
>
> *And thou shalt love the LORD thy God with all thine heart, and with all thy soul, and with all thy might.*
>
> *And these words, which I command thee this day, shall be in thine heart:*
>
> *And thou shalt teach them diligently unto thy children, and shalt talk of them when thou sittest in thine house, and when thou walkest by the way, and when thou liest down, and when thou risest up.*

> *And thou shalt bind them for a sign upon*
> *thine hand, and they shall be as frontlets*
> *between thine eyes.*
>
> *And thou shalt write them upon the*
> *posts of thy house, and on thy gates. "*
> *Deuteronomy 6:4-9*

What elements do you think should be involved in your family devotions?

How do you hope to obey God in the statements of the passage previously quoted?

These things matter and it is when they are consolidated that a marriage can make progress. Let your inner person be a greater focus in your relationship with one another. This is only possible as you learn to develop one another's spiritual life.

> *"Know ye not that ye are the temple of*
> *God, and that the Spirit of God dwelleth*
> *in you?" I Corinthians 3:16*

Always remember that as you put God in the centre of your relationship, you will make progress in all areas because if He is the centre of your joy, everything will hold together. What stands in the centre of your life matters a lot. A marriage, which follows divine order, will know God's favour. God puts His blessing wherever divine order is observed and practised.

Learn to watch over one another in God; *"iron sharpens iron"* and the countenance of a person sharpens that of his friend. The Bible says, *"two are better than one for they have a good reward for their labour"* that is, the two who are busy watching over each other to ensure that they are both doing well spiritually.

In effect, have an agreement as regards church participation. Choose your future local church together if you belong in different places. Understand clearly what your spouse's doctrine or position is as regards the deity of Christ, the authority of scriptures, the sanctity of marriage and the sanctity of sex within marriage. These convictions are not only for you but also for the children whom God will bless your home with.

Above all, in your spiritual life learn to stand together, pray together and agree together. It scares Satan when two who are in love turn to God to form a three-fold cord.

## #8

# Successful Marriages Have A Clear Understanding Of Role-Playing

It is important that as people are going into this great institution, as we earlier called it, establish role plays and understand what the scripture says each person is to do. Along with that, it is important to know what roles both male and female would play in matters related, for example, to the discipline of the children or how household chores would be divided up. If it is a marriage of two loving ones, role-play needs to be very clear.

How do you arrive at major decisions? This

you need to agree on. What happens if you disagree? What about smaller, daily decisions? Do you both have to always meet before you agree on that or can the home move on without disagreement in minor matters?

Role-play is not only related to the daily running of the home. It also has to do with how we fill the emotional cup of our spouse. Successful marriages understand scriptures and therefore, a husband will go out of his way to show affection to his wife so that the wife can respond in love.

Having talked of role play, successful marriages do not always wait; that is check the grey line about who is supposed to do what, but rather they reach out and build their marriage, carrying our projects together irrespective of who gets the glory. Looking at it in more detail, it is important for people to understand that a husband's role in his marriage is established in Scripture to be that of a guide, a guard and a governor.

> *"And the LORD God took the man, and put him into the garden of Eden to dress it and to keep it." Genesis 2:15*

Role-play seems to be a bit clear for most men. Man had position before he had relationship. It is not a challenge for him to know what his calling is. That is why when his position is taken from him, the marriage will be difficult to function properly. Most men derive self-esteem from what they do, their titles, their position. A man is more likely to fling around his complimentary card and remind you of his title more than a woman would.

Women are the opposite more especially when it comes to our relating to the outside world, they remember families we ought to have visited, people we ought to have reached and people whose love we should reciprocate. Women see the loving and tender side of life.

# Successful Marriages Have A Clearly Defined Vision For The Future And Pursue It

*"Where there is no vision, the people perish: but he that keepeth the law, happy is he." Proverbs 29:18*

*"And the LORD answered me, and said, Write the vision, and make it plain upon tables, that he may run that readeth it.*

*For the vision is yet for an appointed time, but at the end it shall speak, and not lie: though it tarry, wait for it; because it will surely come, it will not tarry." Habakkuk 2:2-3*

Vision is life. Where there is no vision, there is no going. Vision is the blue print of your life. It gives direction and purpose to all that you do. The vision is supposed to speak into your destiny so where there is no vision, there is no defined destiny. Where there is no vision, we do not hear what the vision is supposed to speak and therefore, imitation becomes inevitable.

There are many marriages, homes and relationships which hurt because a spouse or both are merely copying what they see others doing. They are not reaching forth into their own destiny to pull out what has been deposited in them and therefore fulfil it. Vision gives light to the future. It gives light where there is darkness. It is compulsive in nature; that is, it makes you just want to carry it out.

In establishing the vision for your marriage, you are also talking of a vision for yourself. When you know your personal vision, the marriage then has something to anchor itself to. Scriptures make it clear that the husband is the head of the home. It is imperative that the husband shares the vision. A vision has to come from one visionary. If it comes from two, it becomes "di-vision" and causes division. The husband shares the vision; they both own and run with the vision. It remains only his until they both see it as their vision.

Vision is necessary to create a family budget or else you will spend as occasion demands and not as a vision directs. In such instances, you will throw your money all over the place without achieving the purpose for which the money is meant. Vision is powerful and where it is pursued, it serves as a magnet to bring to you your expected end. It serves as a magnet to draw you into the land of your expectation.

# #10

# Successful Marriages Put One Another First Before Anyone Else

When morning came and Jacob drew back the curtain of his tent, to his horror, shock, amazement and disgust, he just discovered that he spent a whole night in sexual rendezvous, in a whole night of passion, with the wrong woman! Jacob was probably not the only one who has been waking up or going to bed with the wrong person.

It is possible to be married to a wife who is making love or refusing to because of previous relationships. Some people have difficulty in dropping old boy friends, kissing cousins and uncles that have hurt them. They still go to bed with abuse of the past, unable to release and unable to find healing. We shall talk more about this in a later passage.

This could be very frustrating when a spouse feels that he is not being put first above others. It could be very frustrating when your wife keeps running back to mummy or the husband has difficulty loving his wife because he goes by his mother's opinion.

Successful marriages have become so because they have learnt that this is not just two people living together but is a laboratory where the process of one flesh has started. The scriptures do talk about leaving and cleaving. Couples are given the appropriate adhesive for achieving this. The husband is to love an honour his wife. A woman will go to any length if she understands what she is getting. She will respond to a loving and honouring husband. All a man wants is a wife who understands submission, that it is not a loss of her personality and that there has to be one captain of the boat.

Putting one's spouse first gives marriage direction. Both can then run as if the vision came from both their souls.

## #II

# Successful Marriages Share A Healthy View Of One Another's Relations

In-laws and out-laws: relations are important. They are the ones who raised your spouse but none the less, many have out of zeal and desire to protect their son or daughter hurt the marriage they have gone into.

Successful marriages have learnt how to develop a healthy view of their spouse's relations without allowing them to control their destiny. There are different types of problems, which can come up.

First among them of course is immature parents. These kind of parents keep close ties with their children, unnecessarily imposing laws and rules also wanting to know how things run in the marriage of their children because they are still suffering from Oedipus complex - a disease that makes a person not want to release a son or daughter.

Unhealthy relationships can also come up when the spouses themselves depends on one of the parents for economic deliverance. That is why no matter how economically sound it is, it is unwise to be started in business by your father of mother in-law. It is also unwise to go and live in an apartment with them or belonging to them, even if it is for a short period. The damage done by such economically convenient arrangement will remain in your marriage for quite a long time.

Further sources of damage of relationships come from what parents transfer to their children emotionally. A woman, for example, has difficulty accepting affection from her husband because she probably has never seen it from her father and every time her husband has gone an extra mile, she thinks he is faking it. In the same vein, a heavy handed mother produces a son who over reacts when his wife asks for a simple thing.

Only heaven knows how much damage is caused by emotionally unbalanced parents to their children, particularly domineering mothers, poor role models, over-aggressive, passive, nagging or domineering fathers. They damage their sons and make them feel that is how to get everyone in order. This attitude leads to some relations therefore being over involved to the point of dictating how things should run, resulting in a hurtful marriage.

An immature wife or husband does not easily see through the control tendency which seems to come up in statement like *"you do not know how much my mother loves you"*, *"you do not really know how much my brothers care about you and this marriage"*, failing to realise that no matter how much they care, they should stay away and show their care by praying.

Parents who like to keep the umbilical cord should sever it after the marriage of their sons and daughters. It should go on record that every unsolicited involvement in the marriage of your son or daughter is a form of witchcraft, which is really the spirit of control, manipulation and domination. Those who are building successful marriages must realise that they have one marriage and it does not include their parents, children, friends or even their church leader (because in some instances, a spouse can be manipulative by making the other spouse feel that they are not respecting spiritual authority by edging out a pastor who wants to be over-involved).

It would not be fair to conclude that all in-law relationships are unhealthy. There are more healthy relationships than mother in-law jokes have allowed. If you have great in-laws, let them know how grateful you are for the work they have done on your spouse. Treat their son or their daughter as an absolute treasure and let them know you thank God for the mother or father who raised them.

# #12

# Successful Marriages Recognise Finance As A Tool That Binds

A healthy understanding of finance is necessary for a marriage to be successful. Modern man is faced with a challenge of earning and in most cases today, the husband and wife go out to work. A healthy understanding of what finance is all about and how to handle it matters a lot. Thus money can either be the strength of your marriage or the source of a lot of argument. It could be the tool for carrying out you vision as a family. On the other hand, the love of it can be the root of all kinds of evil for a marriage.

> *"For the love of money is the root of all evil: which while some coveted after, they have erred from the faith, and pierced themselves through with many sorrows." I Timothy 6:10*

A successful couple has to establish therefore whose money it is; the husband's, the wife's or both, and how much of such money you hope to put away, What your commitment is to tithes, offerings and other various financial commitments in the local church and beyond the local church. What level of income do you anticipate in the future and how do you hope to use excess money you desire? Who pays the bills and who buys the groceries? Who shops for the children's clothes and takes care of repairs? If you both work, how do you manage the income each partner brings?

The above are questions a couple needs to resolve to manage what God has provided. Sometimes, unhealthy views do come up regarding money. Some couples feel that all apart; *"this money belongs to us"*.  They see God as a stranger interested in this thing belonging to us and that He is unfair to ask them to give ten percent in tithes and another extra in offerings.

Other problems could come up in marriage, for example, where there is no plan, the couple's marriage suffers a lot of hurt because of mismanagement and not profiting with what God has provided for them.  It is important to have a working plan.  Ignorance, poor planning and keeping up with the *"Jones's"* has led to a lot of indebtedness and leave the couple broke and hurt.  A couple needs to realise that they are stewards of God's provision and to understand that God is interested in how they manage what He has provided for them. Therefore, part of the operational plan should be first and foremost - to make giving in the house of God your priority.

Be committed to the stewardship of serving the Lord with that which He has provided for you. Recognise and respond to God's command to tithe.

*"And all the tithe of the land, whether of the seed of the land, or of the fruit of the tree, is the LORD's: it is holy unto the LORD." Leviticus 27:30*

*"Will a man rob God? Yet ye have robbed me. But ye say, Wherein have we robbed thee? In tithes and offerings.*

*Ye are cursed with a curse: for ye have robbed me, even this whole nation.*

*Bring ye all the tithes into the storehouse, that there may be meat in mine house, and prove me now herewith, saith the LORD of hosts, if I will not open for you the windows of heaven, and pour you out a blessing, that there shall not be room enough to receive it.*

*And I will rebuke the devourer for your sakes, and he shall not destroy the fruits of your ground; neither shall your vine cast her fruit before the time in the field, saith the LORD of hosts.*

*And all nations shall call you blessed: for ye shall be a delightsome land, saith the LORD of hosts." Malachi 3:8-12*

Be committed to giving your offering as a sign of devotion.

> *"Honor the LORD with thy substance, and with the firstfruits of all thine increase:*
>
> *So shall thy barns be filled with plenty, and thy presses shall burst out with new wine." Proverbs 3:9-10*

Go beyond the tithe and the offering and give towards other projects in the local church.

> *"Therefore, as ye abound in every thing, in faith, and utterance, and knowledge, and in all diligence, and in your love to us, see that ye abound in this grace also.*
>
> *I speak not by commandment, but by occasion of the forwardness of others, and to prove the sincerity of your love.*
>
> *For ye know the grace of our Lord Jesus Christ, that, though he was rich, yet for your sakes he became poor, that ye through his poverty might be rich." II Corinthians 8:7-9*

Having made that which belongs to the Lord a

priority, now set yourself in motion to give and to invest. Invest wisely because a spending pattern is often the cause of poverty or the creation of wealth. It is not the only reason, but it does play a major part. Money truly was made to be spent. Nonetheless, do not be led by your impulse in your purchases or else you will become a debtor in no time.

> *"Owe no man any thing, but to love one another: for he that loveth another hath fulfilled the law." Romans 13:8*

Stay out of debt.

> *"The rich ruleth over the poor, and the borrower is servant to the lender." Proverbs 22:7*

Modern man has glorified debt and made it attractive and acceptable. He lives in a house bought with borrowed money, furnishing is from moneys borrowed, that is, he *"buys now to pay later"*. The clothes on some people's backs and the toys their children play with, and even the car they drive to work are all on credit. Eventually, they have launched themselves on an ocean of red ink forgetting that *"the borrower is the servant of the lender"*. Not only does he make himself the servant of the lender, he launches his children in motion for the same thing. Hence, when his children grow up, they will not depart from it.

> *"Train up a child in the way he should go: and when he is old, he will not depart from it." Proverbs 22:6*

Indebtedness has separated families, hurt relations and has made men and women hurt their marriage by going back to their relations to ask for help. Indebtedness hurts and destroys homes. It is very important to remember that not only should you stay out of debt but also, you should develop a management system which best suits your own home.

In some homes, they have a joint account and in others they have two accounts with each partner taking certain responsibilities. A third method is to have three accounts with each person receiving their income in separate accounts and a third account where they deposit the money they have agreed to use to run the home.

Successful marriages recognise the importance of ironing out this nitty gritty because it could hurt the home and cause it to lose its focus. Budgeting controls spending. Planning for the future is all-important to not only meet your present needs but to create wealth for the coming generation.

It is interesting that while poverty is a spirit whose power and control must be broken, it is also a child of habit formed from generations. Those who create wealth tend to raise creators of wealth and children born in poor homes only often come out as a result of knowing the Lord, the source of all wealth, or developing a strong hatred for lack.

# #13

# Successful Marriages Believe And Express The Highest Trust In Each Other

*"The heart of her husband doth safely trust in her, so that he shall have no need of spoil." Proverbs 31:11*

No institution, organisation or relationship can function outside of trust. Trust is the bedrock of staying together as two people with different opinions, backgrounds, up bringing, heredity and environmental experience come together. Trust is necessary to move on together.

Where there is no trust, every wind which blows carries a reason to be suspicious. Distrust and other types of problems will follow where there is no trust. Assumptions, judgement, evil imagination and verbal abuse follow where there is no trust.

Assumptions, for example, are deadly and if you do not trust your spouse, you are likely to assume their reason for lateness and certain actions until you have hurt the marriage through various verbal vituperations that follow. Therefore, whenever you receive any information, have a lead or a hunch, the information must be reliable and not just a hunch or else it will destroy every trust you have in your spouse and every confidence they have in you.

Trust is also necessary for vulnerability in marriage. In marriage, two people who come together should be vulnerable to each other without the fear of exposure. This gives the ability to be able to heal properly from the past, to handle the temptations of the present and to receive confidence for future challenges.

Where your spouse has not expressed a deep trust and has not been able to open up to their mistakes, their pains, unfaithfulness, etceteras, it may be because of the fear of it being used against them. Complete trust certainly is an ingredient for a good marriage.

We need to let our spouse know that we trust their judgement and their opinion and they will be loyal to us forever. This is because we have esteemed them for what they know.

# #14

# Successful Marriages Pursue The Well Being Of Their Partners Above Theirs

Man by nature is selfish. He looks after himself first before he thinks of others. Survival nature says look out for number one. When we come into the union of marriage, it is recognised that our spouse and ourselves have become one flesh. Looking out for their wellbeing spiritually, emotionally and physically goes without saying.

This has to be an effort and an understanding to be cultivated or else, like we said earlier on, the danger would be neglect and overlooking the other spouse. Relationships are like living things. All living things grow but not all living things are healthy. Relationships need to be well fed and cared for to stay alive and be healthy.

You feed your relationship with your spouse with the things can make it work. Sow the right seed into your marriage; caring for one another, looking after each other and trusting one another. Do not wait until your spouse qualifies before you commit to being unselfish.

> *"That thou turnest thy spirit against God, and lettest such words go out of thy mouth?" Job 15:13*

People in marriage know that giving is receiving. As you keep yourself busy looking out for your spouse's well being, you yourself cannot be neglected. Make your spouse feel they are special to you.

> *"He that hath an ear, let him hear what the Spirit saith unto the churches." Revelation 3:6*

*"Her children arise up, and call her blessed; her husband also, and he praiseth her." Proverbs 31:28*

In effect, learn to praise your husband. Make him feel like he is the best you have ever met amongst men. Let the husband bring gifts to his wife. You must learn to appreciate one another. That way you will make the flame of romance keep burning.

# #15

# Successful Marriages Make An Effort To Forget The Past

It is impossible to make progress if we keep crossing the bridge into the past. Nevertheless, when you marry, you inherit all that a person has been through; their fears, anticipation, tears, pains, insecurities and challenges of life.

Jacob was not the only man who when he woke up, found himself sleeping with the wrong person. We all do the day after the wedding. You wake up with the reality that you now live with the person who you probably thought you knew but are just coming to the point of knowing.

Having said that, it is imperative that the

marriage can only move forward as you both learn to forget the past but, both that which you are coming from and the past you have had together as a couple. The Bible says there has to be a leaving before there can be a cleaving.

> *"And the rib, which the LORD God had taken from man, made he a woman, and brought her unto the man.*
>
> *And Adam said, This is now bone of my bones, and flesh of my flesh: she shall be called Woman, because she was taken out of Man.*
>
> *Therefore shall a man leave his father and his mother, and shall cleave unto his wife: and they shall be one flesh.*
>
> *And they were both naked, the man and his wife, and were not ashamed."*
> *Genesis 2:22-25*

A departure from the hurt and pains of the past is necessary. When one holds to childhood hurts and traumas, progress becomes deterred and almost impossible. To make progress in life, we need to bury the past and leave the past where it ought to be and move on into the future.

Painful experiences with boyfriend, girlfriends, relations, cousins etceteras can become part of our story but should not become what holds us from reaching our full potential. How many have crashed their vision in life on the rock of the challenges they have seen. Drop the uncle who abused you, forget the stranger and cousin when going to bed with your spouse.

How many people have experienced frigidity and the inability to open up to their spouse or find fulfilment in marriage because some things about their spouse reminds them of the person who has abused them.

Forgetting about the past will require wisdom in disclosing certain pasts, which may hurt your future happiness. The maturation level of your spouse in necessary to be clear to you before you open up your past to them. There are people who can just not handle what you have been through and where you have been.

A few years ago Joanna sat in front of me sobbing uncontrollably. She had gone through so much. Her spouse wanted to know of her first sexual experience. When she told him she could not explain all that he was persistent. He wanted to know how it all happened. Finally after so much pressure, she admitted to him that she was the victim of incest. Her father had been the one who slept with her. Little did she realise that that was going to be the ruin of her own marriage. If she had known, she would not have opened that aspect to her spouse.

What would you do if your were in Joanna's shoes or that of her husband? It is important that couples that want to have a successful marriage realise that we must make room for the other person to make themselves naked without being ashamed.

Forgetting the past includes forgiving the past. Marriages become healthy where there is abundant forgiveness. It is almost impossible to live together and make a success of your home if you are not ready to travel on the bridge of forgiveness, constantly going to bed sleeping with dead issues, which you have not resolved. You may yourself be committing necrophilia - sleeping with the dead.

# #16

# Successful Marriages Have Partners Who Do Not Use Points Of Vulnerability To Attack One Another

When we reveal people's weaknesses, we do not make them stronger but the opposite. Remember when you shared the vow *"for better for worse, for richer for poorer, to have and to hold from this day forward"*, you committed yourself to a covenant of openness as well as building one another.

Criticism, defensiveness and contempt will destroy the fabric or stability of your marriage, therefore, when you use what you know about your spouse in moments of extreme anger, disagreement or when you need to make a point and gain the upper hand, you violate the whole purpose of conflict resolution which has been dealt with earlier on.

Criticism often dwells on known areas of weakness. It dotes on what it knows of the person Archille's heel and makes it look as though that is all they are - weakness without strength. A critical tongue may rather be revealing an arrogant heart. While you are busy criticising your spouse, you may just be exposing your own arrogant heart.

Criticism results in leaving your spouse's self-esteem lowered and this will hurt you too eventually. A quarrelsome wife may be asking for attention. If there is constant argument in the house, you need to know the root of it. Why is your wife acting the way she is? Could it be that she has been taken for granted or you have not given her enough notice? The abusive husband who hits out at his wife is totally unjustified but at the same time may have used that as the only way to express the fact that his wife has not joined him in building their home.

# #17

# Successful Marriages Respect Differences Of Opinion But Allow Disagreement

*"Finally, brethren, farewell. Be perfect, be of good comfort, be of one mind, live in peace; and the God of love and peace shall be with you." II Corinthians 13:11*

*"And let the peace of God rule in your hearts, to the which also ye are called in one body; and be ye thankful." Colossians 3:15*

Marriage does not take away your individuality. Two people with opposing views and at the same time points of similarity married each other. It is important therefore to recognise that your difference in opinion will not leave in one day. It might even be healthy for your relationship that you have such differences of opinion. If both people in a marriage always agree on all matters, one of them is in complete compromise.

Value what your spouse has to say and do not shut him or her down because they differ in opinion to you. You were attracted to each other by your points of difference. It may not occur to you immediately that two things pull us to those with whom we share our life - whatever makes us similar and whatever makes us different.

Our points of differences cause attraction, irritation, frustration and then later unity. That point of difference may then become that upon which we build, understand each other and build a marriage that brings glory to God. Therefore, in spite of your points of differences, it is good to talk. If you are unable to talk about your present problems, you will soon have permanent ones.

# #18

# Successful Marriages Have Partners Who Appreciate Each Other More Than They Do Third Parties

*"Wherefore comfort yourselves together, and edify one another, even as also ye do.*

*And to esteem them very highly in love for their work's sake. And be at peace among yourselves." I Thessalonians 5:11 & 13*

*"Let us therefore follow after the things which make for peace, and things wherewith one may edify another." Romans 14:19*

The spouse wants to appreciate you and expects you to do the same. At the same time, he or she wants their individuality and originality to be respected and maintained. People will come your way or you might find yourself in places where you are tempted to consider someone else above your spouse. You need to learn to refuse to let the devil lie to you that the grass is greener elsewhere. If the grass is greener elsewhere, they took care of their lawn. Brag about your spouse in their presence, talk highly of them even if they blush. Let people know how special your spouse is and refuse to entertain images, pictures, thoughts, literature, television and anything else that gives the impression that you can fantasise and go free. If you must compare yourself with your spouse or others with your spouse, it should be to show how you spouse is better by far.

## #19

# Successful Marriages Are Made Of People Who Have Stood Together In The Storms Of Life

This in effect means that having taken the decision to stand together in storms of life, you break the bridge of alternatives in moments when sacrificial commitment is required. To stand together in the storms of life means being ready to work hard to make your marriage a success and burning any thing which serves an escape route from the realities in your marriage.

Challenges are there along with the problem

that people want to build castles in the air and escape when their marriage does not seem to deliver all that they thought it should.

How do you stand together in the storms of life and pull down such alternative bridges? You have got to learn to bring down those castles in the air. Stop waiting for your prince charming to come. He is here and you live with him. His name is your husband or your wife. Live with whom you are sharing the future and build a destiny that will be full of testimonies.

One of the reasons why people end up building bridges of alternatives instead of committing to live together despite the storms of life is if they have set impossible standards for a spouse and the person they married does not meet up to the standard or where the real marriage and the ideal marriage does not seem to match. In such instances escape to the unreal world is what one attempts. They do this by comparing their spouse to others. It is time to get real.

Successful marriages learn to deliberately break all cords that connect them to alternative plans and refuse to use alternative bridges in their relationships.

# #20

# Successful Marriages Have An Ultimate Goal Of A Home Where Champion Kids Are Raised

Children are a heritage of the Lord.

> *"Blessed is every one that feareth the LORD; that walketh in his ways.*
>
> *For thou shalt eat the labor of thine hands: happy shalt thou be, and it shall be well with thee.*
>
> *Thy wife shall be as a fruitful vine by the sides of thine house:*

*thy children like olive plants round about thy table.*

*Behold, that thus shall the man be blessed that feareth the LORD.*

*The LORD shall bless thee out of Zion: and thou shalt see the good of Jerusalem all the days of thy life.*

*Yea, thou shalt see thy children's children, and peace upon Israel."*
*Psalm 128*

We therefore need to appreciate them as the great gift God gives to those who he desires. As born again Christians, we must make an effort to create an atmosphere for their effective nurture. Successful marriages work on making their families a testimony to Jesus Christ. Therefore it is important

➲ to set clear objectives for your children. Let them know what you want them committed to and how you expect them to pursue it.

➲ to know and pursue God's plan for your children. God has a master plan for everyone on earth. What plan has he for your children?

Do not force your personal dreams, which might not be consistent with God's ultimate plan for them.

➲ to beware of inconsistency. Walk your talk and talk your walk. Let your life confirm what you teach your children. Children first of all catch behaviour before what they are taught.

➲ to let love be paramount. Let your children see love from your life.

➲ to mirror your faith. Let your children see the faith you have in Christ and imitate your lifestyle in Christ. A good number of children make lifetime decisions concerning the Lord Jesus Christ from what they observe from their parents.

➲ to teach your children responsibility - Social, family and spiritual. Let them know what your expectations are. Lay the foundations, which your children can build on in the future. As soon as they know what your convictions are concerning how they relate to other people, the die is cast and they end up being a blessing to other people.

➲ to clean up your own attitude because it is contagious. Your children will soon catch it. Let it be that which shows consistency, being positive and being civil.

# #21

# Successful Marriages Believe And Keep To The Spirit And Letter Of The Vows They Have Shared

It is interesting that modern man is ready and willing to say and read covenant words without a plan to keep them. Scriptures are very clear that *"truce breakers, snakes will bite them"* in other word, the consequence will follow. Marriages that are successful are that way because they made a commitment to stay true to the vows they have shared - vows of honour, vows of purity, vows to stand through the storm until both are victorious.

A marriage can be successful as long as you are committed to honour your spouse in every way possible. Show them that you value them and that your spouse is the best thing that ever happened to you. You survive the storms together and remember that you said *"for better for worse"*.

These are some of the reasons why it is difficult to practise and experience a truly fulfilling marriage without the presence and power of the Holy Spirit.

> *"And be not drunk with wine, wherein is excess; but be filled with the Spirit;*
>
> *Wives, submit yourselves unto your own husbands, as unto the Lord.*
>
> *Husbands, love your wives, even as Christ also loved the church, and gave himself for it;" Ephesians 5:18, 22, 25*

The heart of a person deeply honoured is the fertile ground for future blooms. If you want you spouse to truly open up, sow the seed of honour on his or her heart and future blooms will follow.

You cannot divorce what a man is and what he does from his theology. If your belief is faulty, your practise will also be faulty. Are you convinced that the vows you said are necessary? Give to the spirit of it and you will enjoy the bliss which will follow. If a man flaunts the content of the vow he shares, if he has disregard for the scriptures or spiritual truth, it will reflect in his practise and will affect his marriage at such times when he should be doing what the word of God says.

# #22

# Successful Marriage Partners Have Learnt To Celebrate Their Differences

*"Variety"* they say *"is the spice of life"*. God wants you to celebrate your differences and not see them as objectionable. Marriages can be strong on the very bases of our differences. Sameness is boring and not challenging. God celebrates difference. He created a world of varieties. Can you imagine a world where all the birds are the same colour and same look or if all of humanity were the same height? We would have a big problem on our hands.

God created a unique situation where all of

humanity is made up of people of differences. At the time of the writing of this book, it is two years before the world will officially clock six billion inhabitants. There are no two faces that are alike. Even identical twins have points of differences - they are different from each other on all counts, finger prints, the nerves of our eyes, voice modulation, facial looks - all of mankind has differences.

The same thing is reflected in your marriage. You have somehow been attracted to someone different from you because they have a contribution to make to cause your life to make sense. Do not fight that difference but walk with it and work on it. Marriages that are known to be successful have been built on the different background both bring to make this new fusion.

# #23

# Successful Marriages Operate On An Open Book Principle

When things are hidden, suspicions become inevitable and things cannot work. In marriages where each person is open to one another, the marriage could be more successful because the other person can contribute without the fear of being judged. Major decisions are made together in such marriages. Healthy marriages are the product of the ability to accept the other person's view without a fear of contradiction, judgement or without giving the impression that one's view is the best view. There can be several views to a matter. The variety could be a reason to the success of your marriage.

# #24

# Successful Marriages Create Enough Atmosphere For Laughter

If you take life too seriously, the *"ups and downs"* of life will take their toll on you. Marriages where the couples have learnt to laugh and cry together last longer and raise a healthy couple. The Bible says

> *"A Merry Heart doeth good like a medicine: but a broken spirit drieth the bones." Proverbs 17:22*

Psychologists tell us that it takes only a few nerves on the face to smile while it requires two hundred and twenty two nerves to frown.

Frowning makes you age and it increases your pain and releases certain toxins into your body system. Laughter does the opposite - it heals your mind and makes you see the funny side to life.

In the atmosphere where both can laugh, they turn every day's mistake into something to laugh about and not a battle. Laughter brings balance to the serious matters in marriage and the spouse can take things as major as eating the same kind of food three times a day because of financial challenges and still be able to laugh about it. If you cannot place a candlestick on a burger for your birthday party, when plenty comes, you might not be able to appreciate it. At the same time, some couples will be separated by the mere fact that there was a lack.

Laugh at yourself and laugh together. Laughter brings balance to the serious matters of marriage. Do not take things too seriously, relax and know that God is in control. If people cannot relax around you, very soon you are given a name that suggests a tyrant. My wife tells me that one of the things that helps her to cope with my travels to preach or minister is probably some of the funny thing that have happened or some of the funny stories I have told her. When alone, she is able to draw strength from the laughter and funny experiences we have shared together.

# *#25*

# Successful Marriages Have Recognised The Poisonous Effect Of Criticism And Therefore Avoid It

When you got married, you made vows that you would cherish this person. Men are visual people while women are oral. A man needs to stroke his wife with the words he speaks to build her self-esteem. Though a man is a visual person, it builds him up and strengthens him when his wife speaks strength into his life.

> *"Let no corrupt communication proceed out of your mouth, but that which is*

*good to the use of edifying, that it may minister grace unto the hearers.*

*And grieve not the Holy Spirit of God, whereby ye are sealed unto the day of redemption.*

*Let all bitterness, and wrath, and anger, and clamour, and evil speaking, be put away from you, with all malice:*

*And be ye kind one to another, tender-hearted, forgiving one another, even as God for Christ's sake hath forgiven you." Ephesians 4:29-32*

Criticism in marriage is like toxin in the blood stream. It poisons and eventually destroys, making life ineffective. Criticism uses guilt and intimidation to put down the other person and achieve its purpose. Attacks on the personality of your spouse leads to one being critical. You are doing yourself damage by criticising your spouse because you are now one flesh in the sight of God.

A critical tongue of necessity may be a sign of a condemned heart. Criticism is a projection of how the critic feels. Criticism can be in form of

harsh or caustic jokes shared with the intention
to put down the spouse or to get at them.

> *"As a mad man who casteth firebrands,*
> *arrows, and death, So is the man that*
> *deceiveth his neighbour, and saith, Am*
> *not I in sport?"  Proverbs 26:18-19*

# *#26*

# Successful Marriages Keep The Romantic Flame Burning

It does not take too long after a couple have lived together then things begin to be monotonous, repetitive and almost predictable. At such times it is easy to take one another for granted and expect that marriage will just work by itself without you putting in any effort. To keep the romantic flame burning, you have got to do and say what sparks the fire in your spouse.

Men are moved by what they see and women are moved by what they hear. Say the right thing to your wife, let her know how much you love her and how beautiful she is. This develops the self-esteem of a woman. Build the emotions of your husband. Put on the kind of clothes he likes, use the perfume he likes and do the hair style your husband likes. Do not take it for granted that because you now live together, everything is okay and because he is not complaining does not mean he is happy.

Spouses must learn to keep stimulating one another mentally, spiritually and emotionally. There was something about your spouse that attracted you to him or her. There was something which stimulated your spiritual and mental life. Let them know what that thing is so they can keep the romantic flame burning.

Talking face to face is also better than being back to back. No matter what has happened in your marriage and no matter what arguments you have had, whenever you have the opportunity, let it be face to face. Settle your differences and move on instead of turning your back on each other. Keep the fire quenchers out. Fire quenchers of necessity are those things that quench the romantic flame. Keep them out.

Keep also from just being together. You did not get married to just look at one another. You got married so that this person can bring all the joy you have always wanted and you can in the same vein reciprocate. Surprise and creativity can spark the fire of romance. Surprise your wife, go home with a bouquet of flowers, and buy a new dress. Never come from overseas without something new or something special. Give her a reason to look forward to your coming home. Be creative with what you do. You do not have to sleep the same way you always slept. Put your legs where your head used to be and your head where you legs used to be. Just be a person that makes fun out of difficult situations.

Unconditional love and acceptance is also necessary to keep romantic flame burning. Years down the road your spouse is not the same size or looks you married. That is why the Bible talks of *"accepting one another in the beloved"* so that your relationship is not based on physical attraction only but on the inward person.

# #27

# Successful Marriages Recognise The Person And Influence Of The Holy Spirit In Marriage

*"And be not drunk with wine, wherein is excess; but be filled with the Spirit;*

*Speaking to yourselves in psalms and hymns and spiritual songs, singing and making melody in your heart to the Lord;*

*Giving thanks always for all things unto God and the Father in the name of our Lord Jesus Christ;*

*Submitting yourselves one to another in the fear of God.*

*Wives, submit yourselves unto your own husbands, as unto the Lord.*

*For the husband is the head of the wife, even as Christ is the head of the church: and he is the saviour of the body.*

*Therefore as the church is subject unto Christ, so let the wives be to their own husbands in every thing.*

*Husbands, love your wives, even as Christ also loved the church, and gave himself for it." Ephesians 5:18-25*

Man, by nature, probably has certain comparatives with other animals. Monogamy is not natural for animals and is probably not natural for the fallen man. This is because monogamy is probably a spiritual thing. In effect to be properly monogamous, you need to be in tune with the Holy Spirit who is able to make you truly commit your spirit, soul and body to one person.

This is the reason why the unsaved keep getting a divorce as it requires a true commitment to Jesus to be able to stay successful and allow the influence of the Holy Spirit have an effect on your life. You see nothing in the nature of a man wants him to live with this man or this woman who seems like an alien for the next fifty years. Your spouse is different, strange and sometimes they surprise you almost every day.

There has to be a bonding or it will not work and this bonding is only possible when the Holy Spirit is in it. Other than that, if the commitment is only between two imperfect people, like we said earlier on, and God is not in the middle, it just will not work. Therefore we are told in Ephesians 5:18 to be filled with the Spirit. It is interesting to note that the subsequent teaching, which follows that verse, is about role-play in marriage. It shows in effect that the Holy Spirit and marriage go together.

Taking it a step further, create a mission statement for your marriage. Have a spiritual goal which you are both committed to and your seek the help of the Holy Spirit to make it happen. If your marriage will succeed, you need the wisdom of the Holy Spirit who has been from the beginning. He was there when your spouse was made.

*"Who knows a man save the spirit that
is in him."  I Corinthians 2:11*

Therefore, since the Holy Spirit knows your spouse better and He, the Holy Spirit, is the greatest teacher, submit and surrender your marriage to Him.  He will teach you what way you ought to go and what thing you ought to do to make your home a success.

*"The grace of the Lord Jesus Christ, and
the love of God, and the communion of
the Holy Ghost, be with you all.
Amen."  II Corinthians 13:14*

This verse says and the communion of the Holy Spirit be with you all.  Communion comes from two words - *"common union"*.  Our common union must be under the influence of the Holy Spirit.  Where it is, the marriage will succeed. We are not alone.  A greater hand leads. Marriages where the Holy Spirit is an active participant will certainly succeed.

# #28

# Successful Couples Celebrate One Another's Strength And Successes

Successful marriage spouses do this. It is important to understand that the strength and the success of your spouse is not intended to be used against you and should therefore not be a threat to you. Spouses do feel threatened if they have a problem with their self-esteem. This in effect means that just as the success of someone outside your marriage could threaten you, that of your spouse is likely to threaten you if they do not know how to manage the glory of it.

The wife, for example, must realise that she

must not hurt or maim her husband with her success. The husband should not be egotistic as he derives his self-esteem, many times, from his achievements. If the wife is an achiever, she needs to know how to play her cards right and manage herself despite all those achievements.

A healthy man should be proud of a gifted wife and should boast about her, talk about her wherever he is and encourage her to go on further in achieving. If she can sing well, let her know and possibly arrange for her to take some more singing lessons. Be the rock behind her and the strength for her giftings. Give your spouse a healthy appreciation of the good attributes they possess. Do not let them hear praise from outsiders alone. Never allow anybody to outpraise your wife. Never allow anyone to praise your spouse more than you do. Let most of the appreciation come from you. Praise your spouse for their successes. Let them know how proud you are for their achievements.

A healthy and rewarding marriage is the product of appreciating one another's good qualities. When this is done, it lifts your spirit and encourages you to achieve more, as your therefore know that you live in an atmosphere of acceptance. No one is ever motivated to achieve more by the negative. This is where people hurt by the negative that what has been used to motivate them.

Make your home a place where you brag about each other and let the world know you are proud of each other's achievements. That way, you stay humble and you reap the harvest of one another's achievement without the threat it is likely to bring.

# #29

# Successful Marriages Are The Product Of Healthy Communication

In previous pages, I had said that communication in marriage where it is open and possible helps the relationship. Not only should communication be open, it needs to be healthy. Blame games and criticism only hurt a relationship. Unfortunately, the blame game started in the Garden of Eden when Adam blamed the wife and the wife blamed the snake.

Successful marriages always aim to restore, encourage and edify one another. They do not deny the presence of challenges and problems but they do face these situations with a mind to overcome and to be victorious. In like manner, in your marriage today, recognise the enemy's desire to sabotage whatever you say or do. In communication, there is encoding and decoding. Encoding is the message you have loaded into words you have used. What the wife hears is called decoding or vice-versa. It could be the wife who encoded and the husband who decoded.

The sad thing is we have an enemy who hates marriages. Demonic spirits hanging around tend to want to take what one person said and load it with mis-information before it gets to the other person even though it is in split seconds. We have to recognise the fact that we may not be hearing our partner right before we are up in arms. Communication needs to be healthy and part of it is opening your heart to your spouse, but not opening up what will hurt the relationship. It is no use sharing a past, which may destroy what you are trying to build, so focus on that which brings health into the relationship. By that we mean that there are unhealthy ways of communicating.

Communication can be unhealthy if you talk too much or if you do not talk at all. They are extreme opposites; too much talk or not enough talking. Too much talking refers to sharing the unnecessary to the point that you may not have recognised that your spouse is still at a level of maturation which may require waiting a while before they will be ready for the things which you may want to say. Also, the fact that your spouse needs you to communicate with them regularly does not mean you should share other people's private matters.

Women have a habit of personalising information, taking it in from the side of their emotion, therefore, it could result in the personal damage of your wife if you share with her unhealthy things you know about others.

Healthy communication includes telling the truth without exaggeration and telling the truth in love. It may be true that your wife snores or it may be true that your husband is sloppy but there are ways of communicating one's feelings and have the emotions and self-esteem of the spouse still intact.

Remember that in communication those angry responses only provoke similar actions.

*"He that is slow to wrath is of great understanding: but he that is hasty of spirit exalteth folly." Proverbs 14:29*

*"By long forbearing is a prince persuaded, and a soft tongue breaketh the bone." Proverbs 25:15*

*"Be ye angry, and sin not: let not the sun go down upon your wrath:*

*Let all bitterness, and wrath, and anger, and clamour, and evil speaking, be put away from you, with all malice." Ephesians 4:26 & 31*

So, it is important to check out your response before it goes out. Either way, silence may be golden but it is not so in marriage. Silence in marriage is very frustrating. If the spouse requires to know a thing and it is not unnecessary, you need to open up to your spouse. Strengthening communication could be done by sharing your thoughts, your fears and your concerns so that your spouse knows where you are, meets you where you are and builds the marriage together with you.

Follow that with giving your spouse undivided

attention. Action speaks louder than words and lifts your spouse's spirit. It makes them know that they matter a lot to you and that you are not trying to frustrate them. Listening coupled with long responses will do a lot of healing for any hurt that exists in your marriage. It will also help your spouse to move fast from the past they are coming from.

> *"He that answereth a matter before he heareth it, it is folly and shame unto him." Proverbs 18:13*

# #30

# In Successful Marriages The Spouse Places A high Value On Filling Each Other's Emotional Cup

In healthy marriages, the spouse looks out for the other person. We all have our invisible emotional cup. We started having it filled from our home background. Some cups are empty, some are half full, while some are well filled. The way we treat our children, the atmosphere of love, appreciation, acceptance and non-judgemental upbringing we raise them in determines if their emotional cup is filled. In every man is still a little boy and in every woman is still a little girl. The spouse can become the source through which this cup is perpetually filled. Certainly a marriage will succeed where the spouse makes the effort to fill the emotional cup. Filling the emotional cup is possible by being a ready listener.

> *"Wherefore, my beloved brethren, let every man be swift to hear, slow to speak, slow to wrath:" James 1:19*

The spouse has things to say and you should be their first supporter and greatest fan. Know what your spouse likes and give them a lot of it. Let them have so much of what they have always liked which you can afford to provide. Never let a day go by without letting your spouse know they are loved. Men need to hear it as many times as possible because a man is the *"head"* person while the woman is a *"heart"* person. Let your husband know how much you value him and how much you respect and adore him as a person and his gifting.

Marriage is like farming. It only gives back what you sow into it, therefore it is important that you fill your spouse's emotional cup, as you will be the one who benefits from it the most.

Delight your spouse by giving surprises. Do the unexpected. Buy the unexpected. Never come back from long trips empty handed.

Give accolades in front of an audience. Do not just tell your spouse you appreciate them when you are alone with them or behind them. Say it in their presence and fill their emotional cup and moreover touch them. Kiss, hug and just fondle them. A touch lasts longer on the mind than all the money in the world. It fills the other person's emotional cup.

Give them surprises and do the unusual. Always remember that love making really starts when you wake up in the morning. The mind of the other person could be prepared from the morning or be shut from waking up.

## *#31*

# Successful Marriages Know Their Enemy And How To Defeat Him

*"I am going to divorce you!"* Randy said as he paced the floor of the front room of his house. Suddenly his wife burst out of the kitchen screaming her head off *"Go ahead make my day, I will let you know that I may be a Christian but I will not take nonsense"*. Unknown to Randy and his wife Janet, that in the supernatural realm a battle was raging between angels and demons. One wants the success of this marriage and the other working hard to see to its demise.

Successful marriages recognise the enemy and how to overcome him. The reality of spiritual warfare cannot be over emphasised particularly as it relates to marriage. We do know what the enemy could use; hatred and disagreements could increase in a home to the point where they do not want to see each other whereas love could have covered a multitude of wrongs.

> *"Hatred stirreth up strifes: but love covereth all sins." Proverbs 10:12*

Further more, the enemy can use unforgiveness and the presence of sin in a marriage. Hence when people refuse to forgive their partner, they fail to provide the bridge upon which they themselves will travel one day.

Eventually the couple begins to talk of divorce as if it is an easy option. They fail to realise that while the law courts have made divorce easily accessible and while divorce has also become a twentieth century challenge for the church, the consequences are always there. A divorced couple never really leave one another a man may leave your life physically but the emotional challenge the trauma and in the case where there are children in-between, the impact of the marriage stays with you.

> *"And the Pharisees came to him, and asked him, Is it lawful for a man to put*

*away his wife? Tempting him.*

*And he answered and said unto them, What did Moses command you?*

*And they said, Moses suffered to write a bill of divorcement, and to put her away.*

*And Jesus answered and said unto them, for the hardness of your heart he wrote you this precept,*

*But from the beginning of the creation God made them male and female." Mark 10:2-6*

*"What therefore God hath joined together, let not man put asunder." Mark 10:9*

To make the fight between couples even worse, sometimes they begin to deny one another their sexual rights. Satan takes advantage of this and that increases the gap between them.

*"Defraud ye not one the other, except it be with consent for a time, that ye may give yourselves to fasting and prayer; and come together again, that Satan tempt you not for your incontinency." I Corinthians 7:5*

> *"And unto the married I command, yet not I but the Lord, let not the wife depart from her husband." I Corinthians 7:10*

Where there is no love lost, our relationship has gone sour and the wife is unable to fulfil her obligation to her husband neither is he ready to show his wife how much he loves her.

> *"Submitting yourselves one to another in the fear of God.*
>
> *Wives, submit yourselves unto your own husbands, as unto your own husband, as unto the Lord." Ephesians 5:21-22*
>
> *"Husbands, love your wives, even as Christ also loved the Church, and gave Himself for it." Ephesians 5:25*
>
> *"So ought men to love their wives as their own bodies. He that loveth hid wife loveth himself." Ephesians 5:28*
>
> *"Nevertheless let every one of you in particular so love his wife even as himself; and the wife see that she reverence her husband." Ephesians 5:33*

➲ Why do these arguments take place in marriage?

➲ Why is the enemy attacking Christian

marriages?

Firstly, **because he hates the family unit.** The strength of a nation is determined by the strength of each unit. If the family unit is strong emotionally, spiritually and socially, it reflects on a national level. Satan knows that the best way to disintegrate society, the best way to tear the spiritual fabric of society is to attack the family unit.

Secondly, **he hates the future of successful marriages.** It is obvious that successful marriages produce successful children who end up themselves repeating a successful marriage. In most cases, Satan attacks such a home because He knows if he cannot get the couple themselves, he will get the children eventually.

**Satan also hates the faith of a successful marriage.** The home of such believers is a good image of what God can do when two aliens come together and are bound together by a stronger cord and a stronger love that the one they can see in the natural. Such homes belittle Satan's strategy and power. He therefore does all he can to frustrate and to stop them from fulfilling their purpose.

**Successful marriages experience attack because Satan hates their friendship.** In our previous teaching we established that though successful marriages are made up of men and women who may have lived together for quite a while, friendship has not diminished but has strengthened by experiences of life. There is no other reason why Satan manipulates Randy to tell his wife that he is going to divorce her other than the fact that he hates the family unit.

**Successful marriages are under attack because Satan hates the fire of romance in Christian homes.** Today's homes are built mostly on the physical. Satan is working hard to keep it that way. Successful marriages have kept the fire of romance that is not motivated by the natural but has its roots in the love of God. Remember at the end of the day that Satan's plan is to kill, steal and to destroy all the blessings in a Christian home.

> *"The thief cometh not, but for to steal, and to kill, and to destroy: I am come that they might have life, and that they might have it more abundantly."*

*John 10:10*

He is an enemy with a strategy and method of attack that is very devastating.

> *"(For the weapons of our warfare are not carnal, but mighty through God to the pulling down of strongholds;)*
>
> *Casting down imaginations, and every high thing that exalteth itself against the knowledge of God, and bringing into captivity every thought to the obedience of Christ. " II Corinthians 10:4-5*

On the other hand, it is probably healthy for the Christian home and for successful marriages to have an enemy because;

➲ your enemy keeps you on your toes.

➲ your enemy keeps you fighting.

➲ your enemy makes you want to achieve.

➲ your enemy causes you to give the best to what you have because you know you stand the chance of being ridiculed.

A knowledge of the battle the Christian marriage faces is not enough it is important to know the weapons we can use to fight the encroachment of evil. Christian marriages are not shielded from the battles of life but they can face the next attack with;

⊃ **THE PRAYER OF AGREEMENT**

> *"Again I say unto you, That if two of you shall agree as touching any thing that they shall ask, it shall be done for them of my Father which is in heaven".* Matthew 18:19

> *"Likewise, ye husbands, dwell with them according to knowledge, giving honour unto the wife, as unto the weaker vessel, and as being heirs together of the grace of life; that your prayers be not hindered".* I Peter 3:7

The prayer of agreement is a powerful tool for receiving blessings from God. In no other arena is it more applicable than within the Christian home where these two persons have now become one flesh on the bases of the covenant which they share. When God looks at them at the altar of prayer, he sees one flesh - two personalities but one flesh.

## ➲ HARD WORK TO MAINTAIN A FAMILY ALTAR

The family altar is similar to the prayer of agreement but you do not apply the prayer of agreement at all times. The family altar is the place where both husband and wife (and as the Lord blesses, with children) meet before God.

The family that prays together stays together. We read in scripture of kings who broke down the altar of God and elevated to idols. Work hard to see that the family altar is given priority and place in your marriage because praying is winning. If you do not pray, you are playing and if you are playing, you are straying.

## ➲ THE WEAPON OF THE BLOOD OF JESUS

> *"And they overcame him by the blood of the Lamb, and by the word of their testimony; and they loved not their own lives unto the death." Revelation 12:11*

We are told of the battle that raged in heaven and how archangels could not in their power overcome the devil. The joy we have is that the blood of the lamb that was slain at the foundation of the world, who John the Baptist acknowledged, the lamb worshipped in the book of Revelation chapter four is made available to us to apply for the protection of our homes.

In the book of Exodus, it is shown that the physical application of the blood of the Passover was great protection against the onslaught of the spirit of death. Much more will the blood of Jesus Christ do greater things than the blood of bulls. We take great comfort in the scripture that says that it is the blood that speaks better things.

> *"And to Jesus the mediator of the new covenant, and to the blood of sprinkling, that speaketh better things than that of Abel".  Hebrews 12:24*

If any weapon works for the believer against the onslaught of the enemy, it is the weapon of the blood.

## ⊃ THE NAME OF JESUS

Jesus teaches that;

> *"And whatsoever ye shall ask in my name, that will I do, that the Father may be glorified in the Son.*

> *If ye shall ask any thing in my name, I
> will do it". John 14:13-14*

"*Whatsoever*" connotes anything. When the Christian family realises that the enemy is behind the unrest, the tendencies of the children to rebel, the problem between the couple, when the Christian family realises that the little toothpaste that caused two weeks of argument is not really the problem but that there is a puppet master whose presence is sometimes not acknowledged or who does not want his presence to be known, when the Christian family realises the source of its attack, the battle is half won. The family must go to every war with the name of Jesus.

> "*The name of the Lord is a strong tower:
> the righteous runneth into it, and is
> safe". Proverbs 18:10*

Therefore, successful marriages are the way they are because unlike Randy and his wife, they do not waste their energy arguing about what is not or giving the enemy a foot hold which he turns to a stronghold. They see behind their greater battles a puppet master. They go to the Lord in the prayer of agreement, working hard to avoid all strife and rebuilding their broken family altar where they first met the Lord and all the burdens of their heart rolled away. They stand behind the blood which avails for those who trust in God but lastly, they hold unto the name of the Lord knowing that His name is as good as His very presence and He tells us that whatsoever we ask using His name, it shall be done for us.